Turtles All the Way: Poems

by

Rosemary Douglas Lombard

Finishing Line Press
Georgetown, Kentucky

Turtles All the Way: Poems

Copyright © 2016 by Rosemary Douglas Lombard
ISBN 978-1-63534-052-5 First Edition
All rights reserved under International and Pan-American Copyright Conventions.
No part of this book may be reproduced in any manner whatsoever without written permission from the publisher, except in the case of brief quotations embodied in critical articles and reviews.

Publisher: Leah Maines

Editor: Christen Kincaid

Cover Art: Pancake tortoise Willow, "Me"

Author Photo: Lynn Nakamura

Cover Design: Rosemary Lombard

Printed in the USA on acid-free paper.
Order online: www.finishinglinepress.com
also available on amazon.com

Author inquiries and mail orders:
Finishing Line Press
P. O. Box 1626
Georgetown, Kentucky 40324
U. S. A.

Table of Contents

Hatching 1
Other Realms 2
Agate Beach: What I Kept 3
Wafford's Eyes 5
Box Turtle Eyes the Harvest Moon 6
Aesop's Winter Race 7
Haunted Garden, with Farfel Lombard 8
Flick of an Eyebrow 12
Trillium 13
Time Flies 14
The Pancake Tortoise: *Malacochersus tornieri* 15
Tortoise Out of Africa 16
The Pancake Tortoise and the Gorilla 19
Pancake Tortoise Likes Some of the Golden Lions 20
Angel Dancing 21
Thirteen Ways of a Turtle Looking 22
Puzzle 25
I Want to Tell You Something 26
Ask Me, Says the Turtle 28
Communication 29

*To the ancients, the turtles, on their not-so-slow march toward extinction, just as science is beginning to recognize that they are "Surprisingly Smart"**

May our species be their help in these times of need.

*New York Times, November 19, 2013, D-1, D-5

HATCHING

Egg tooth cracks white shell
Turtle peers out to the world
Everything so big

OTHER REALMS
for Lynne Cox

Serendipity alone showed me the turtle
swimming in the distance as I floated, languid,
beyond the maelstrom of the surf.

A stray wave turned me his way,
and I saw him come to life in a frolic of youth
like a dream or blued mirage,

a butterfly below the waves
who surged to the surface for air,
then dipped to skim by rainbow-tinted rocks

where anemones flowered with tentacles waving him on
beyond their high-tide mealtime,
their twice-daily picnic so dangerous to prey.

With my eyes and mind on the turtle's play
my ears missed the warning growl of the sand and the waves,
and a rogue spewed me out unawares.

I hit the beach with force,
the gravity of my terrestrial self returned,
and I wished for the freedom allowed by a space
like the wavering depth of the turtle's world,

to fly into valleys and fly into heights,
escaping in play to extra dimensions
like the eagle above who soars through the air,
the turtle who soars beneath the waves; but I

am a visitor, foreign to the height beyond trees
and the realm of the sea. I must go home
to plod with my ground-bound feet on the earth:
above the water and underneath the sky.

AGATE BEACH: WHAT I KEPT

Past the bulbous holdfasts of kelp
drying above the lapping lines
where sanderlings peck, then skitter escape

from waves, we amble along
where still-wet sand squishes
beneath the gurgles of our rising feet.

It's called Agate Beach, my sister says.
You'll see why. So my eyes follow her eyes.
Focus, she says. Find the gleamier ones,

translucent and smooth beyond the matte
of conventional stones. They're scattered by tides
above the ash and acrid detritus of bonfires

and over the acre of beach. So easy.
My pockets pouch out with one, then two small weights,
then more, and I add a bag to hold them all.

But my agate focus fails. Among the pebbles and sea stink
of rotting kelp and broken bits of plastic and crab,
a small piece of driftwood stalled on sand

distracts my scan, and I lift it close and turn it
before my new jeweler's eye. A tortoise
gazes back—its head a near-perfect sculpture

but for unseen scales, their age now burnished
to the softness of a thimbleberry leaf.
The nostrils are tiny emptied rock holes on the beak

and the polished eye a tiny gray pebble
imbedded in an almond hollow.
The darkest, deepest crack

curves up in a smile, a tease of my ignorance
of its unknown years in ocean, perhaps over seamounts,
through forests of seaweed, its mother tree tossed

in storms, rolling and scraping at last
on jutting outcrops of rock till tortoise broke off
from the bottom-battered log. It floated and dipped,

bouncing alone on its journeys, dancing in waves,
smoothed more each season by rounding
rocks of the bottom and the beaches.

From the moment I saw it waiting for me
at rest by an agate, I abandoned the stones
for the mysterious smile of the seagoing tortoise

made by the ocean and delivered to me,
my emblem of the turtles home alone,
waiting for my return.

> Sing us the songs of the sea, small brother,
> of roaring surf and grinding sand.
> Tell us, tortoise, of your journeys far and yet farther
> in the heights and the depths of the ocean,
> then turning finally back to land.

WAFFORD'S EYES

Wafford, your eyes
are midnight skies of miniature worlds
far from our planet's city lights
and the vapor of our air.

Each shining bead
reflects a single star but hides
your mysteries behind their blackness.

Tell me, tortoise the size of my hand,
how can I read their secrets?

BOX TURTLE EYES THE HARVEST MOON

Shorn short of the tulips of spring,
the field by the windmill looks out toward the east,
where gray-blue hills shield our Oregon valley
and gray-blue clouds sit in rest along the ridge
where we look for the harvest moon.

A pointless drive, Shelley, I say,
to abandon the sheltering trees of our yard
to see the harvest moon.

But a ghostly pink disk peers through the scrim of the clouds,
an omen perhaps in the play of our lives,
where the fates pull the rope for its rising,
and I catch my breath as wandering wisps
inscribe dark stripes as straight as a staff
over the face of the harvest moon.

It's there! I say to Shelley the turtle.
She stares for a moment, then balances tall in my hands
and sways and sways to the left, then right, far left, far right,
her back legs stretching and retracting again and again,
her eyes on the harvest moon.

Tipping back, she touches her nose to mine,
an Eskimo kiss of "thank you," I think,
then turns herself turtle, resting her roundness cupped in my palm,
the stripes of her plastron displayed to the sky,
but her eyes on the harvest moon.

AESOP'S WINTER RACE

Like slow tortoise, degreed for persistence,
the snowflakes slowly race
toward piled higher, piled deeper
than ever before in this place.

Multiple times for multiple feet,
slow and steady they build their case
as they trod on weed and fallen tree.

Like rabbit, cars forget the old race
and seek a sheltered place to sleep,
the road abandoned, tracks effaced,
while snowflakes earn their Ph.D.

HAUNTED GARDEN
with Farfel Lombard (three-line stanzas)

Winter shower stops.
Reptile, turtle, talks a poem.
Home west delights him.

Gentle hammer taps—a beak.
Turtle seeks words on the wall.

Chickadee sings
eating our sunflower seeds.
Pretty—dark black and white.

Towhee crashes the seed dish.
Seeds dashed everywhere!

Robbers dream of meals:
things plot, money plot.
Fortune knife by moon.

Clouds extinguish the moonlight.
Danger creeps and flies through them.

When trees make shapes of winter secrets,
garden sways my haunted step.
Turtle flies inside.

Lamplight banishes shadows.
Fear, locked out, settles to sleep.

Poem cracks under lamplight,
curls up hurt.
Beside the window I sing.

The window stands at attention.
Light, dark, visions: You may pass.

Turtle looks grouchy.
Out, garden noises and voices!
Have a massage.

The breeze lifts the leaves.
They rustle together, laugh.

Squirrel performs a moon step,
mirror of moonlight cycle.
Act drives laughter.

Could Armstrong do that moon step?
Too small for mankind.

Squirrel performs a giant leap,
choice movie staging for Neal,
easy for a squirrel!

Astronaut says he's light, too—
but only in space.

A sight hold to mind:
Remember Earth's sunflowers
greeting the blue sky,

the yellows, oranges, and reds
screaming Earth's appeal.

Red garden.
I color red fire space!
Nothing is dark!

Bring on the lights at nightfall.
Let our reds be seen.

Apple red excites eye.
Lunchtime, although midnight's past.
Owl doesn't feast!

He shrugs his feathers,
flies off to darkened gardens.

Silent feathers glide to frog,
deliver owl its dinner.
Burst of death-bright red.

Blood eddies in quiet pool,
ventures into the dark stream.

Welcome the light.
River runs by home garden—
let yellow mirror flow.

Blood of night has gone downstream.
Owl floats in satisfied sleep.

Frog yesterday sang love.
Surprised by death, his fire is out.
Eternal slumber.

The first croaks of early spring
the last croaks for lover frog.

Luminance of moon,
bright hole to heaven's teasing,
lies on empty pond.

Yes, "The gods must be crazy."
Cruel humor: lunacy.

Study fire's way.
Fire tells a hard kind of story:
writing disaster.

Reds to blacks to new green life.
Dawn extinguishes fire fear.

Turtle reads your laugh
at garden midnight fears!
Together understand.

Life is fears and laughs.
Sunshine evaporates tears.

Season of fear leaves.
Silent shoots sign early spring,
garden smiles again.

Violas, pieri survive.
Turtle smiles, taps his poem.

"Haunted Garden" is modified from renga or renku, old Japanese party games in which participants alternate in contributing three- and two-line stanzas, linking content to the prior contribution and, at specified stanzas, referring to specified traditional topics such as season and moon. The poem remains in its game form, unrevised.

FLICK OF AN EYEBROW

Finger your name in my dust.
Let me see your flick of an eyebrow

and your glance at the edge of the rug.
How much do you think I care?

What matters is the white flash of trillium
exploding the shade below somber skirts of cedar,

the promise of a golden-tipped crocus
and pink-sepaled bud to shatter the winter palette,

the gilding of a morning moment when the dawn light of spring
finds my bedroom window and cracks its joke between the blinds,

the subtle smile of a pupil-dark eye from a handful of friend
I begin to read by long acquaintance,

the surge of her tortoise muscles a motor against my hand
that somehow lifts my feet to follow her will,

and the moments a happy conjunction of words slides together
amid the wonder of near-infinite combination.

TRILLIUM

Behind drooping branches of the western red cedar,
degrees darker than where I work excising weeds,
white arrests my glance,

first a patch or two on this year's berry leaves,
a hint of action above, and I peer
through branches to find no nest.

Below, though, nestled near the massive trunk,
is white my eyes had sought not long ago,
when even the leaves I hoped would return were missing.

Trillium! It's here!
I thought it gone the year the tenants
brought their unpermitted, digging dogs,

>   but trillium, more faithful than Fido,
>   returned, and it returns again.

I run for tortoise Dittow and kneel as we look down.
Three pointed petals, a trifoliate whorl,
a pattern of threes again,

and—odd, another bloom complete,
its symmetry perfect but opposite,
two petals only, two leaves, not living up to its name:

trillium, three; tripartite, a trinity, three.
Name follows form as form follows function.
Isn't three the way it should be for trillium?

>   Three plus one is lucky for clover.
>   Three minus one, who can say?

TIME FLIES

I watch for the time flies,
for those rankling pests dressed
in black or iridescent green,
who, like me, wait for the days of warmth

when I can settle below the bending grass
and scratch myself into drying dirt, my plastron
in comfort, and accept again the solar gain
from slivers of sun that brighten the gold of my carapace.

I know the time has not yet come,
though I sit in my garden window
and each day watch the glass so close by my beak
as the Blackseed Inn's birds proceed through the year.

Beyond the eaves, the cherry, and cedar,
the geese surely mark the sky, but I cannot see the beyond
to tell the time their true arrows point;
and their travels precede the turtle days' heat.

I have only the summer timekeepers, flies,
whose flight plans of time are never like those
of the arrow, straight forward, or a circle of pips on the dial
that measure in minutes, not seasons.

But when a flash of black first flies by my window,
or when I hear its housebound, exasperating buzz,
I forgive it its indecorous habits
and rejoice that my summer has come.

"Time Flies" plays with the underlying ambiguity of the phrase "Time flies like an arrow," which fluctuates in meaning like the reversal images swinging in our visual perception between, say, a duck and a rabbit. In this case, time flies as nouns are the house flies, which in their emergence mark the clock of a watching turtle's outside season.

THE PANCAKE TORTOISE
Malacochersus tornieri

Malacochersus
Tortoise looks out from the rocks
Kilimanjaro

Lava black and stark
Wears a shrinking cap of ice
Kilimanjaro

Malacochersus
Ventures to tawny grasses
Hidden tawny shell

Malacochersus
Noticed by hungry lion
Sprinting tortoise hides

Malacochersus
Squeezes herself in the crack
Lion paws but leaves

Malacochersus
Tortoise looks out from the rocks
Kilimanjaro

TORTOISE OUT OF AFRICA

I fought with his turtle, the Boy complained,
and so I must be sold.

Fighting? Why not? Uprooted from under
my African rocks, stacked with turtles all thrust
like me into a binding, blinding box, closed

and dark as the hand that plucked me from my life,
a hand that should feel in me the pain of his people
sent in chains from home.

Our journey of fear was torture:
One flat tortoise pressed above the next,
plastron to carapace, carapace to plastron,

unsheltered heat, the noises of men
bouncing, bouncing us up and down
with the rhythms of their steps,

then jolts and hums of rolling machines,
screaming at times as if caught by hyenas,
and one that roared, more chilling than the lion.

I festered for eternities in its freezing stomach.
As those empty hours passed,
a deluge from time to time descended,

falling off our rock-like edges,
carapace to carapace, tortoise to tortoise,
dropping and pooling in the bottom of the box,

engulfing dark links of excremental sausage,
their acrid stink the memorial to a meal—
for fear was now my only food.

Bump! *squeal* . . . stop. Then silence.
My body at last was still,
and I dreamed of placid rest beneath my rock.

But again the jostling and bleats of machines, but different
noises of men. Again a stop, and someone cut open the box.
Lightning struck in, so bright it made me close my eyes.

A hand, pale and pink, grabbed my shell and set
me in a box with vertical rocks on all the sides, impenetrable,
like hardened air, ghost stone unseen, as if it were not there.

Others, now boxed too, looked out
and tried to scale invisible cliffs
or push their bodies through to roam

at large, but who could escape from that?
Who could return to golden grass
and rocky hills of home?

I stretched out my neck, so stiff, and noticed
a pool. Water, oh water! It called to my thirst.
I crept to it and touched its impregnable edge.

Then light disappeared, a magical sight:
from day to night in a moment.
Exhausted, I slept.

A first dim glow signaled morning.
The men and ones with higher noises came
and blazed the magic sun awake. How, I did not know.

Some came by and looked at my box,
mouth-blowing out their noises—odd—
like "...t-t...so *ffft*." I remembered the sounds

repeated but wondered what they meant
as I studied the strangely soft and stretchy heads
with unfamiliar shapes of fur and met their animal gaze.

A smaller one, the Boy, had bright, excited eyes,
and soon I traveled in a box again. His home grass
was cold, and overhanging trees were not like home.

A stripèd turtle thought it his and tried
to drive me out. Of course I fought! My anger roused
against the world fell clattering on his shell.

I waked each night at moonrise and patiently tracked the time:
the full of the moon to the full of the moon to the black
of the moon. The travel box appeared.

I was to be sold again.

THE PANCAKE TORTOISE AND THE GORILLA

Quake the tortoise is enamored
of a gentle stuffed gorilla,
a silverback fully three feet in stature,
for Quake, a giant in size.

She pushes against his soft plastic nose,
a chelonian gesture of greeting or friendship or love.
She nestles against him,
his fur soft as clouds on her neck skin so delicate
it seeks out the softness of velvet.

PANCAKE TORTOISE LIKES SOME OF THE GOLDEN LIONS

Tortoise neck loses its turtleneck fold,
all its slack lacking, whenever the prize,
a dandy golden dandelion,
reaches skyward on its slender stem

but impishly evades the maw
spread wide of golden tortoise,
whose stretching jaws cannot quite reach
and hold that precious gold.

'Lion swings and dances off,
shoved aside by touch of jaw
or breath of breeze, a miss just off the edge of the rim
as the basket reaches for the ball.

If tortoise were at home in Kenya
on his hillock above the plain,
who then do you think would be hunting whom,
and who would dance away?

If a golden lion called,
tortoise would dance the running dance,
legs alive for his life and askitter like lizard,
bound for his hole by the kopje's boulder ball.

ANGEL DANCING
for Angel

> *Poetry of the foot*
> —John Dryden

Our angel dances airborne with no pin
(though a pinhead may be classic for one kind).
In her scan I see her float within
the eternal mystic blackness of the night.

Angel has the other kind of head,
this one attached to her curvaceous neck
and fitted with a brain that, joyful, leads
her transit system, me, with feet and beak

as she pushes prancing through the atmosphere
not on a pin but on my friendly palm,
her strength transmitted to my permissive feet
as she explores the world without with calm.

An angel who dances on the head of a pin
must not be a turtle, nor even her kin.

THIRTEEN WAYS OF A TURTLE LOOKING

1.
At the foot of a forested hill
box turtle watches and waits
by the side of the road. Cars,
partly animals, pose no danger?

2.
I look down at her, and turtle
becomes the box of her name, eyes
and all of her tucked in.

3.
The pink tall animals
make many-flavored sounds.
Does a turtle mind
save an image in the dark?

4.
Turtle creeps under maple leaves matched
to golden stripes. A surreptitious eye
tells a turtle's truth—her philosophy of hiding:
Watch, she says, but be not watched.

5.
In hand the turtle, Diode, loses wildness.
Her curious eyes seek novelty. Human high,
she learns the joy of flight.

6.
Her limbs become paddles and pushers.
Her push, pull, press of my hand lead my feet
to follow her motion and gaze as she turns and climbs—
my human hubris abandoned on the floor.

7.
She regards the marks on the spines
of the books. Diode, do you decipher the details?

8.
In the garden she turns to the colors of roses and lilacs
and nestles her head in bright petals and scents.

9.
Shell arching high shields turtle
from torture of teeth.
Closed, she survives the attack.
Wait. Don't peek now.

10.
From my hand, this mother of many
peers under leaning bunchgrass.
We search for her napping daughter.

11.
Turtle son climbs toward me
and gives me The Look.
Pick me up, it says.
Please let me fly.

12.
Box turtle studies puzzle pieces
jumbled in the jigsaw box,
dips down to choose one,
points to its place in the blue.

13.
Diode steers with sudden verve
to fix her eyes on a sprawling spider plant;
she holds her stare, pivots, and directs
me to another plant—a pair now—then more.
With houseplants all found, she visits twenty mirrors.
At each she stops and stares.

Oh, Diode!
Though reptile,
you looked, you classified,
and then devised a way—
a turtle's charade—
to show us what you know.

PUZZLE

The last piece of the tree frog slides into place.
We feel like creators to make him appear
from a thousand shards of rainbow,
lifeless in a box.

In the light his eyes now spark
with the reddest of the reds,
and he perches, tensed as if to spring,
a return to the darkening jungle—

or where the jungle was, now fields and huts
and men bearing frog-catching nets.
There is no jungle there or here:

here only a wall for the three-foot frog,
where he could hide behind the door
and peer over my dimly lit room

brushed the colors of leaves,
with flowers and songbirds in frames
and vines painted green on the mirror;

or we could take this frog apart, piece by piece,
till he's lifeless again in his cardboard casket,
as frog by frog his kin disappear from ponds and trees,
their flashing pigments gone, their clicks and calls now silent.

I study his eyes. I think they are fading.

I WANT TO TELL YOU SOMETHING
after a line by Ruth Stone

I want to tell you something with my voice,
how long I studied ways to push my buoyant breath
and shape its whispers with my tasting tongue—

sibilants, fricatives, plosives, a sopranino squeal
(its voiced excitement rarer in my more placid age),
pronounced with hints of meaning, a shorthand expressed in sound,

sometimes guessed by my human tutor, who towers
over my ground-bound form. Her own voice flows,
its vowels mellifluous, bearing syntax precise in the speaking.

I want to tell you something with my limbs,
the way she gestures wide with her hands,
though my four feet are pulled to earth until I'm lifted high.

Aloft, my forearms canoe, my figurehead beak sets sight,
my back legs push or pivot a finger, a signal to help me turn
or swirl a gentle *pas de deux*, the swing of waltzing in air.

She follows my lead—a miracle—so I can explore: perhaps
a corolla that opens to color and scent, beak-tap
a mirror (or maybe ten or more), the marks on the spine

of a book, a hanging balloon I swipe to spin
with my feet or my beak; or on my keyboard's keys I lean
my chin to voice my chords below her *obligato*.

I want to tell you something more with my beak,
how I touch it to paper taped to the glass, press
my hard horny nose, and stretch my neck

to slide my first line, swinging off to the left
or right as she holds my body still and lifts
her other hand, tracing over my invisible ink.

I want to tell you something you may have guessed already:
that a turtle's brain can break out from the box you assumed
constrained and sing beyond its given lot of instinct.

ASK ME, SAYS THE TURTLE
after "Ask Me," by William Stafford

You meet me steering down the woodland trail,
secure in the hands of my tutor. You look
in her eyes and ask her what I always hear:
Does it know you? And what does it eat?

I say, ask me. I am not an it.
Ask why I lead her, how I inspect
the flowers, how I bury my beak
in their centers, how I learn their names.

Ask me about my early years alone
far east of here by a mountain, a creek, a forest,
a road, where I found my own food and my shelter
and shivered in fear at raging thunderstorms.

Ask me how, when I go with her
to the slopes of a mountain's forest,
the coolness of the spring-fed creek
penetrates beyond my shell, and why

I stay and drink and drink;
how I found a slug in the grass
that she didn't see, brick red and huge,
my dream! and consumed it, every bite.

Ask me how long we two have been friends
and how we learn each other's ways.
Your asking would give my eyes a smile.
It would hold tight in my mind.

I cannot tell you here or now, but come with me,
and I will push my beak to mounted paper
and slide it along for you to record my lines.
I will show you the columbines I love.

COMMUNICATION

Box turtle Diode ambles up the forest path,
sometimes on her own four feet, but most times leading
mine or tilting in her swaying dance.

She pushes my palm
and air-canoes ahead or stops,
swerving aside with swings

of her head, inspecting and choosing
a flower to frame for a photograph.
When the screen is just so, she nods,

and I push the camera's button.
Sometimes she sits on the path, relaxed,
and watches: a turtle's observing way.

Now the path is getting steeper, and I
am breathing hard from chatting while climbing.
Do you remember David Attenborough's

nature shows? I say to Di, *how he hiked,
then huffed and puffed like me in between all his talking?*
[Yes], motions Diode with a left-jerk of her head

to the message-board thumb of my stretched-out hand.
But as forest thins and blue and sun sneak through,
the incline levels off. I settle onto a moss-covered log,

while the birds we've missed below
in darker forest show us their voices.
In shining treetops two unseen songbirds

I've never heard before sing duos,
each in his own twittery way.
One I can whistle back,

a garbled rendition, yes, but the other?
so high, complex, so capricious
my mind can't hope to catch up.

Diode, at my feet, attentive,
her head angled up toward the birds
from brown, sun-dappled leaves,

hasn't moved a muscle since we settled here.
Now the birds are farther off,
and gusts of wind are shaking the canopy.

Trees say to each other, Sway.
We sit still and listen.

Acknowledgments

I thank those who have previously selected poems that appear in this book: Dorothee Lang, editor of *BluePrintReview* (Germany), in which "Haunted Garden" first appeared; Laura LeHew, who selected "Puzzle" as an Oregon Poetry Association contest winner, thus in the anthology of winning poems, *Verseweavers;* and Artists' Milepost, which selected "Puzzle" for a reading and exhibit of environmental poems and art, Unnatural Acts: Crimes Against Mother Earth, at Denizen Gallery, Portland, Oregon.

I am also grateful to the Spring Creek Project for Ideas, Nature, and the Written Word at Oregon State University for Trillium Project residencies for box turtle Diode, her daughter Angel, and me. Our projects centered on Diode's experience revisiting the wild after 43 urban and suburban years with humans compared to Angel's vacation to the wild as a captive-bred turtle. Diode's return led to my "Communication" and "Ask Me, Says the Turtle," the former printed in our first report, *A Captive Turtle Revisits the Wild: A Human-Turtle Collaboration,* May 2014, limited distribution, the other posted online by Peter Sears, Poet Laureate of Oregon.

I thank Farfel Lombard for permission to include our collaborative "Haunted Garden."

I thank the poets and writers—too many to name—who make up western Oregon's rich literary community by their writing, reading, teaching, and generous friendships. For certain poems, I appreciate prompts by Paulann Petersen ("Agate Beach"), Marie Buckley ("Thirteen Ways of a Turtle Looking," referencing Wallace Stevens), and Peter Sears ("Ask Me, Says the Turtle," referencing William Stafford's "Ask Me"), though I take responsibility for turning key ideas on their heads.

And, finally, I am grateful to matriarch Diode and the other turtles of our cognitive behavior lab, who turned all of our lives turtle from what they might have been.

Rosemary Douglas Lombard chose her education at Lewis and Clark College (*magna cum laude*), where her favorite professor was William Stafford; Indiana University–Bloomington, where she approached the end of a doctoral program in musicology before being distracted by the behavior of turtles; Columbia University, where she spent a summer studying Renaissance music and poetry in an NEH seminar for college teachers; and San Francisco State University, where she turned into an animal behaviorist. She has taught in universities, run a biomedical library, edited scientific manuscripts, served as a naturalist and environmental educator on San Francisco Bay, and more, but mostly she treasures her decades of exploring turtle cognition in her independent laboratory. She presents readings, lectures, and lecture-demonstrations at universities, conferences, museums, libraries, coffee houses, galleries, and elsewhere. She serves her community as co-director of the Conversations with Writers series. She has won awards in poetry and nonfiction and has published literary work in journals and anthologies including *Bay Nature, Work Literary Journal, Verseweavers, BluePrintReview,* and *Blog Carnival>Language>Place*. Her creative nonfiction work in progress, a book about her companion/laboratory turtles' empowering quest to learn to communicate with the humans, is called *Diode's Experiment: A Box Turtle Investigates the Human World*. http://ChelonianConnection.blogspot.com

www.ingramcontent.com/pod-product-compliance
Lightning Source LLC
LaVergne TN
LVHW041504070426
835507LV00012B/1323